Calligraphic Meditation
for Everyday Happiness

ILCHI LEE

Calligraphic Meditation
for Everyday Happiness

ILCHI LEE

BEST
LIFE
MEDIA

BEST Life Media
6560 State Route 179, Suite 220
Sedona, AZ 86351
www.bestlifemedia.com
877-504-1106

First hardcover edition: December 2015
Library of Congress Control Number: 2015952879
ISBN-13: 978-1-935127-84-0

TABLE OF CONTENTS

Author's Preface

Early one quiet morning, I lift my brush. Flowing and dancing, the brush moves on its own, creating shapes and meanings. Whenever I put my mind into my brush like this, I feel the joy of creation, of escaping from some confining mold.

My life reveals itself freely moment by moment. I love this space and time for sending my spirit and energy flowing into the world.

Early this morning, I dream of a world where all are happy. I am grateful we all have good souls that long for the good of all. People who are making their bodies comfortable and controlling their breathing, listening to the good voice within, people gladly choosing the life that voice wants, giving their all to practice what they have chosen…

I dedicate this book to those who exist in beauty as the light and hope of the world.

Some of the calligraphy in this book depict scenes and images that I wanted to express, while other show Chinese characters. The Korean word(s) for the Chinese characters and their meaning are written below them.

A New Beginning

Last night's darkness, no matter how black,
cannot stop today's sun from rising.
It's a new beginning.

Byun: Change

See the morning sun rising.

Today's new sun drives away last night's old darkness, bringing a new day.

More than anything else, it is a symbol of intense hope and renewal.

Since heaven and earth appeared, those who can begin their days with the reverent consciousness of the cosmos, which has continued without missing a single day, will never be brought low by one or two reverses.

Those who often watch the sun rise and set open their eyes to the cycle of life, though no one tells them of it, and obtain wisdom from that.

Like a farm boy learning naturally of life as he watches the fields beginning and ending the cycle of a year.

Take part in the cosmos boisterously welcoming the morning. When heaven and earth awaken, understand the quiet yet majestic sign of their awakening, and, arising with it, bow respectfully to the sacred morning.

Between sunrise and sunset, live the day's majesty with greatness.

This day, today, is not a repetition of yesterday. Today is a sacred time in which I can create something new, a time that cannot be violated by the remorse, regrets, sadness, and frustration of yesterday.

Today is a new day.

Happiness Is a Choice

Do not entrust your joy and happiness to others or your external environment. Happiness coming from the outside is like sugar water; you will soon feel thirst. Go to the spring within you that never runs dry. Bring your joy and happiness up from that spring.

Bok: Luck

The only way for us to check whether we have enough inner joy and happiness is to try using them. When you try using them, you will feel and know.

Try to smile consciously, even if you have nothing to be happy about. Then a calm, quiet joy will arise within.

Smile not because you are joyful, but because, by smiling, you create joy.

No matter how unfortunate the situation you face may be, if you choose happiness consciously, you will come to know the plentiful happiness already inside.

Recognize that joy and happiness exist within you, and continue to develop them infinitely by using them constantly.

If you think, I can't find happiness no matter how much I search for it, then borrow some happiness. Make it so that the god of happiness has no choice but to come and find you to collect on the happiness loan he gave you.

Try smiling quietly when you open your eyes in the morning. Or try saying out loud, "I'm happy." In that moment, the energy of happiness will gather around you. Remember that feeling and express it whenever you get the chance.

What's important is believing and recognizing for yourself that infinite joy and happiness exist within you.

Choose joy and choose happiness immediately, moment by moment, without delay.

Try borrowing an advance on happiness immediately, right now. We can use, without limit, the card of happiness we have, for it has no expiration date and no credit limit.

This Moment, Now

Nothing at all from the past can damage the
novelty and sacredness of this moment, now. We
can always realize this moment, now, and create
something new.

Nothing exists but this moment, now.

The past has passed, no matter how beautiful it may have been.

The future has not yet come, no matter how wonderful it is expected to be. All is illusion, except for now.

And nothing exists in the now. In the now there is neither joy nor sadness, neither achievement nor failure.

Now is a time that cannot be divided into minutes or seconds.

Within a moment that cannot be measured by the concept of time, we can encounter our true selves.

Nothing I had up to a moment ago has any relationship with me in this moment, now.

Whoever we were, whatever circumstances we faced—such things are not absolute.

Return to the seat of self-existent life without beginning and without end, obtain new strength, and start the life you want now.

If you awaken to this moment, now, then every moment is a new beginning, a new opportunity.

Between Heaven and Earth

Below, the earth firmly supports me. Above, infinite space is open to me. Standing on two feet, I feel my body linking heaven and earth. Standing on these two feet, I walk the path of the human being below heaven and above the earth.

In Joong Chun Ji II: Human bears heaven and earth

Now, stand upright on your two feet. If possible, take off your shoes and socks, and stand barefoot. Adjusting your posture, feel the soles of your feet pressing firmly against the floor.

If you stand there, quietly focusing on the soles of your feet, at some moment you'll feel the weight of your whole body.

Find that feeling of your body's weight being delivered fully, without obstruction, to the soles of your feet.

Feel your body's weight being transmitted to the ground through the soles of your feet, and feel the power of the earth supporting that weight.

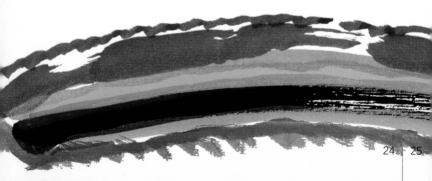

This is the feeling of vibrant life. A vibrant feeling of being, that I am living here now, and a sense of humility and gratitude for the earth supporting my body and life—all this wells up from somewhere deep within.

The stronger the feeling in the soles of my feet, the stronger the feeling in the crown of my head pointing toward the sky.

Below, I feel steadfast legs, and a lower abdomen filled with energy. Above, I feel my chest refreshingly open and my head cool and clear.

Love overflows in the hearts of those who stand here on their two feet, embracing heaven and earth.

Your Perfect Refuge

Set your body down comfortably. As you control your breathing, let your mind watch your body. Tell yourself, "It's all right." Then your soul will become more comfortable, and your body will gain new comfort and strength along with it.

Ahn: Being comfortable

You can obtain genuine strength and rest within yourself. Your body is your refuge and your energy generator.

Your perfect refuge is inside your body.

When you're shaken and confused, go into your body.

If you relax your body, control your breathing,
and tell yourself, "It's all right," with those
words your soul will gain strength.

You cannot find true rest outside yourself,
no matter how far you may drag your body.

Our souls gain greater strength from
comforting ourselves than from being
supported by others.

Life Is Nothing

There is no greater comfort and blessing than the knowledge that life has no meaning. Your life has nothing like a fixed destiny or purpose. Therefore, all you have to do is assign your own life meaning and value, and devote yourself to creative activity for realizing that value.

Mu: Nothing

Life has no meaning at all.

Life does not have some purpose fixed in advance.
It is truly meaningless.

You must fully awaken to this.
But do not break down over the emptiness
of a meaningless life.

Understand that complete meaninglessness is the
point where infinite creation begins.

When you awaken to true nothingness and all the
empty fictions you once thought of as "Me" disappear,
then self-existent life without beginning and without
end finally touches your heart.

When you don't know that your source is nothingness,
you experience all kinds of battles and divisions to
realize your self, which is a fiction.

When you know that the source of being is nothingness, you abandon your attachments by realizing that everything you thought of as "Me" is, in fact, a temporary construct created by your true essence.

Freedom springs and genuine creation begins where attachment has disappeared.

Understand deep in your bones that life has no meaning. Assigning meaning and value to your own life, immerse yourself in creative activities that will make that value real.

This is the life of the enlightened:
Dreaming dreams even while knowing that everything is nothingness, and giving your life to realizing those dreams, doing your best to live for the values and meaning you have chosen.

Dragon Energy

Call forth dragon energy with the power of
your mind. You have nothing to fear, no reason
to hesitate. No worldly tempest can block the
dragon's rise. Create to your heart's content, riding
the whirling energy of the dragon.

Yong: Dragon

Great creation is impossible without risk.

If you want security, forget about doing new things or taking great strides into the unknown.

Nothing is won without risk and challenge. Many of the world's great creations were realized amid occasionally life-threatening risks.

The things we think are limitations are often, in fact, illusions.

Don't imprison yourself within limits you've set in advance. Don't make your limits absolute.

Permit yourself the energy of the soaring dragon.

Open wide the iris of your consciousness. Have the will to challenge yourself and encounter a new world.

Only when you challenge yourself and crash against obstacles can you awaken the energy of infinite creation hidden within.

Surfing Life's Waves

Life is so beautiful and worth living, despite all
those awkward steps and frequent falls, because
we have the will to get up again and keep walking,
because we have within us a lava-hot passion
for life.

I drink a cup of single-leaf tea late in the afternoon. A slightly bitter taste is followed by sweetness. It's a delicate flavor, sweet while bitter. How deep and wide is the gap between the sweetness and bitterness contained in this one cup of tea?

Joy and sadness exist together in the cup of life. We cannot fill the cup of life only with joy because we hate sadness.

Like single-leaf tea, which has a deeper flavor for its bitter taste, happiness and joy shine in the background of the anguish and sadness of life.

Open wide your heart and accept all the experiences of life. Don't let any moment go half-lived. Live with greatness even in moments of sadness and pain.

It is no shame to trip and fall as you walk the path of life. Just get up and continue on your way.

Shout boldly: "Oh, you joys and sorrows of life, come one and all. All experiences that come to me, whatever they may be, I will make valuable and beautiful."

Those who have truly become the masters of their lives surf life's waves of joy, anger, sorrow, and happiness. From these they make their lives into works of art.

The Observer's Eye

We are surrounded by countless thoughts, emotions, and habits, both inside and outside, that can tangle us up. But by watching ourselves, we can use our eyes and minds to escape. When the eyes of the observer come alive, we can become true masters of life.

In our minds are countless spiderwebs binding us. Thoughts and emotions and habits . . .

Outside our minds, too, are countless spiderwebs hindering our freedom. Institutions and systems and social practices . . .

Becoming an observer is about finding eyes for seeing these webs. If you see, you'll know; if you know, you'll develop the power to choose without being entangled in such webs. Creation happens through choice.

We are so used to living in these spiderwebs that, at first, observer consciousness is strange. To remain in this consciousness, we have to practice a great deal.

Once we experience continuous change through observer consciousness for a while, we realize that observer consciousness is not some special state—it is, in fact, the most natural state of consciousness.

The greatest characteristic of observer consciousness is realization: seeing your situation without becoming mired in it.

Unless you have observer consciousness, you don't have the freedom to separate yourself from your situation. In other words, you identify yourself with your situation.

When you have observer consciousness, you recover the power to separate your situation or environment from yourself. You recover the power to choose.

An observer creates her own life by making the best choice in any situation without being led about by her conditions or environment.

Brilliant Solitude

Within deep solitude, which cannot be shared with anyone else, we see the essence of the loneliness experienced by all life. In the moment we see this loneliness, a deep compassion and love for everything in the world warms our hearts.

Knowing that we are fundamentally lonely beings is wisdom. That knowledge gives us strength because it is truth.

Paradoxically, when we are completely lonely, we can feel the whole beyond the individual.

As the empty fields of winter teach us fullness, as the gaunt trees of winter remind us of warm passion for life, so, too, solitude teaches us connection and mutual understanding.

We have an earnest desire to connect and understand other lives because we have absolute solitude.

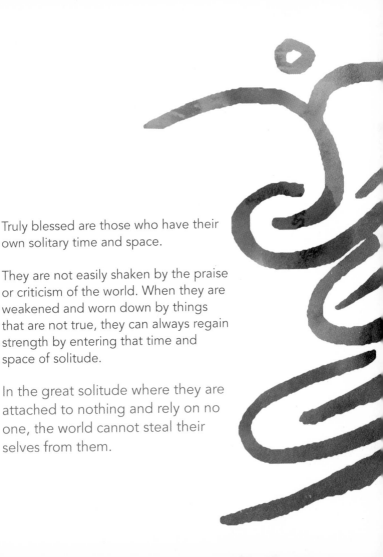

Truly blessed are those who have their own solitary time and space.

They are not easily shaken by the praise or criticism of the world. When they are weakened and worn down by things that are not true, they can always regain strength by entering that time and space of solitude.

In the great solitude where they are attached to nothing and rely on no one, the world cannot steal their selves from them.

The Canvas of Your Life

Using your emotions like paint, draw a beautiful picture on the canvas of your life. Express and use to your heart's content all your emotions, going with the flow of your soul, with the feeling of your life.

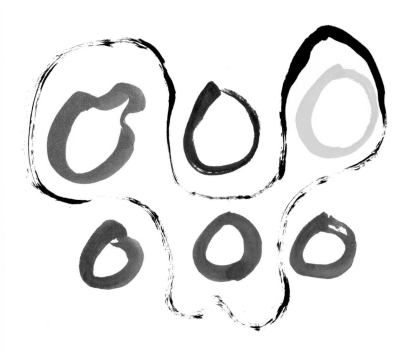

With the brushes of desire and emotion,
humans make countless strokes on the canvases
of their lives before going on their way. Mixing
and separating, those desires and emotions
create a picture of life.

While you live, desire and express your
emotions to your heart's content.

Freely paint with all those emotions—
love, joy, sadness, loneliness, fear, solitude,
despair, hope.

But do not become mired in emotion.
Feel your soul.

Let your soul use your emotions; don't let
your emotions use your soul. Go with your
soul's light, with your soul's dreams. Using your
emotions like paint, draw the beautiful picture
you desire.

Then you will experience true freedom and
peace without losing yourself in countless
emotions.

The Pulse

Concentrate until you encounter yourself, until you feel your self-worth. Concentrate until it hits you deep in your heart how beautiful and great you are. Enter deeply, deeply into the sacred rhythm of life until even the self you once felt to be so great completely disappears within massive energy.

律呂

Yullyeo: Rhythm of life

When distractions fill your mind, stop what you're doing, place your hands comfortably on your knees, and shake your head gently from side to side. This is the method of meditation called Brain Wave Vibration.

By repeating these simple movements, you can create healthy vital phenomena within yourself. In no time your lower abdomen will become warmer, saliva will collect in your mouth, your eyes will brighten, and your head will clear.

When your thoughts and emotions are calmed and a completely empty tranquility comes to you within the vigorous vital phenomena created by your body, you will suddenly have a realization.

You will awaken to how precious and beautiful a being you are. You are not better or worse than others, but an absolute, self-existent being incomparable with anyone else.

Now you have found your own unique rhythm of life. As you are immersed in and feel a sense of complete oneness with yourself, the life within you blooms fully. By becoming one with the rhythm of life, your body recovers health, happiness fills your heart, and your

soul experiences deep peace.
What's important is finding and
frequently expressing your rhythm. In
the process of expressing yourself, you
develop an affinity for yourself, and your
self-immersion deepens.

If you only imitate the rhythm of others
without finding a rhythm of your own,
though you may be able to make an
exquisite copy, you won't be able to
engage in genuine creation.

Find your own rhythm, and
confidently go with that rhythm.
When you become one with the
rhythm and flow of your own life,
you will encounter the rhythm of the
universe that bestows harmony and
order upon all things: the pulse of the
cosmos, Yullyeo.

Encounter the Void

An openness, purity, and wholeness lacking nothing and with nothing in its way—this is the void and the true heaven. The void is who we really are.

Chun: Heaven

The void is not far off. It is within and without all things. The void is smaller than the smallest thing, and bigger than the biggest thing.

We encounter the void every moment through breathing. We accept the void by inhaling and become one with the void by exhaling.

The energy of the cosmos fills the void. As we breathe, the numinous energy of the cosmos circulates in our arms and legs and light shines in our eyes, illuminating the darkness of ignorance. A large-hearted, peaceful energy overflows in our hearts, healing the world.

When you accept and become one with the void, your heart opens like the heavens, your mind shines bright like the sun, and all attachment and foolishness vanishes.

When we encounter and become one with the void, we can be genuinely free, and we can use infinite energy to foster infinite creation. That is who human beings truly are.

A Brightening

The Korean word *Hwanhamnida* contains the meaning "bright." Your face becomes brighter and more cheerful, as the word suggests, when you say it out loud. When your heart is heavy, don't fret. Try saying, "Hwanhamnida!" out loud, and you will feel yourself lifting.

Hwan means "righteous and just mind; bright mind."

Hwan is also the mind that communes with all. It is the mind that knows we are all connected through one life. Our faces become truly brighter and clearer when we know that we are one with heaven, earth, and all the life in between, and when we seek to work for the good of all.

You become more hwan, brighter and clearer, if you frequently say the word, hwan.

You cannot properly say "hwan" with a sad or frowning face. Only if you're smiling can you say "hwan" the way it should be said.

When things are dark, say, "hwan." Don't be mired in worries. When worries come to mind, quickly say, "hwan!" and take action immediately. New doors will open before you.

No one and no system of the world can judge your bright, clear value.

You have a bright, clear mind, a bright, bright consciousness, always whole and self-existent.

As you say "hwan," remember that bright, clear mind, and return to it.

Just One More Step

When you think you've reached the end of your road, take another step. When you think you've done your best, try just a little harder. Just one step creates a new path, and just one attempt can launch extraordinary results.

II: One

Have you ever lacked interest in a task and, failing to double-check your work, had to spend vastly more time and energy on it later? Have you ever given up on something halfway through and then thought over and over again about what you missed out on?

Have you ever felt the pain of estrangement from others because, hesitating, you failed to take the first step toward them? Have you ever had lasting regrets because you couldn't bring yourself to understand and care for another person one more time?

Probably all you had to do was make just one more attempt.

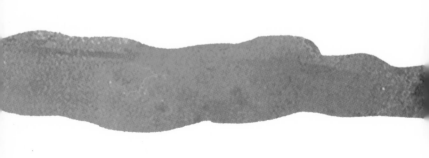

Take interest and check once more; be the first to take one step closer; try to understand once more; make one more attempt.

That willingness and attitude—that once more—can truly make all the difference.

The Body in Bloom

My breathing happens on its own, though I don't
even try. My heart knows when to beat, though
I don't worry about it. My body maintains order
even amid disorder, creates stability even amid
change, and exhibits perfect circulation, rhythm,
and balance. My body is a playground where life
takes a stroll.

Heaven enters us, by way of our noses, through air, and earth enters us, by way of our mouths, through food. We are beautiful flowers blooming, rooted in heaven and earth. Just as positive and negative poles meet to create bright light, so, too, our lives shine brightly with a light that heaven and earth create together.

I don't have a life of my own; life created by heaven and earth together expresses itself through me.

My body is a flower brought into bloom by life, a phenomenon caused by life.

Those who know that the source of life is found in heaven and earth realize deep within their hearts the true meaning of the words "You and I are one."

Air that entered my body a moment ago and flowed through my warm blood now flows into the chest of the person beside me. Water brought up from the ground by a tomato a few days ago is now in my body.

All living things are connected as one through heaven and earth.

Those who, through direct experience rather than ideas, realize that our lives are maintained by heaven and earth cannot do things that hurt heaven and earth.

Joy of the Soul

Heaven has given us hearts too great and warm to love only a few people. We pursue the love of the soul, which transcends our little selves, for we have hearts more than able to embrace all humanity and the world.

When I've done something good without hoping for any reward or without awareness that I've helped someone, there is a joy that rises in my heart. It is the joy of the soul.

Unconditional peace, spontaneous joy and satisfaction, and a little smile coming from the heart are my only rewards, but the joy of the soul is a joy all my own, whether or not someone recognizes it. That joy is absolute and long-lasting.

The joy of the soul never runs out, no matter how much you may share it.

For it is a mutual joy obtained by helping others do well, not a joy taken from others or won in competition.

When our joy of the soul grows, we come to know a great love that embraces compassion for all things in heaven and on earth.

At first, we develop a desire to help those nearby; when that heart gradually grows, we come to have concern for the whole world, not just human beings, and we begin to think about how we can help.

When we have such an attitude, the life within us looks up to us in respect.

The Alchemy of Gratitude

Gratitude is a technique of the mind that anyone can learn and develop. When your experience and understanding of gratitude deepen, you'll know that it simply means being grateful for everything, in any circumstance whatsoever. Every moment of life will be filled with gratitude, and you needn't try hard to find it.

At first, gratitude must be looked at to be seen, must be sought to be found. Find something to be thankful for, even if you feel it's insignificant. We all have something to be thankful for.

If you really think you have nothing to be grateful for, then be thankful you were born a human being. Be grateful that you are still breathing and that your heart still beats. And be thankful that the sun rose today, that a new season has come, and the trees are green again.

If you have true gratitude for even one thing, at some moment thankfulness will rush over you like a wave.

When thankfulness matures, then appreciation—temporary, conditional, and calculating—gives way to unconditional, sustained gratitude.

Such gratitude takes away from our lives' complaints and dissatisfaction, anxieties and worries, and brings in their place infinite positivity and peace.

Train yourself to be thankful, whatever your circumstances. Let gratitude fill your whole mind so that thankfulness overflows into your whole life.

If your heart is filled with gratitude, you can't live halfheartedly. You can't use tricks or do cowardly things for your benefit alone.

When you are grateful, you show full devotion in whatever you do and do your best no matter whom you meet.

A holy mind comes out of a grateful heart. Gratitude is an alchemy of the soul everyone should practice.

Enlightenment

Who am I? What do I want? These two questions are different, but, ultimately, one question lets you find the answer to the other. If you find the answers to these two questions, your life will start to reorganize around them.

Do Tong: Being enlightened

Who am I? What do I want? Do you have your own answers to these questions?

Quietly close your eyes, and try talking about what it is you genuinely want in your life. Try to feel how your heart reacts.

Who am I? is not a question about your job or bank balance. Don't be satisfied with rational or formal answers. Ask yourself seriously and honestly, again and again, and, sooner or later, you'll hear the voice of your soul. The true answer will come to you, breaking through the thick curtain of your ego, which is made up of your name, job, personality, and similar things.

These are the two oldest and most frequently asked questions in the world. No matter how many people have asked them, and no matter how many people claim to have found answers, these questions are always new.

Even if you know it with your head, the answer will become your own only if you discover and experience it for yourself. You can say that stars in the night skies of summer are beautiful.

Love, at times, is like the most painful poison, but we can say that it is the most beautiful emotion human beings can experience.

But if you have never actually had a moment of awe looking up at the stars in the sky on a summer night, if you don't have the experience of love for someone welling up in your heart, then you know nothing.

Ask yourself these fundamental questions.
Never fear being shaken.

You don't need to worry if you don't get an answer right away. The heart asking those questions is important. The longing to know is important. When warm morning sunshine illuminates our windows, we naturally awaken from sleep and open our eyes.

When your heart grows hot with the longing to know the answers to the fundamental questions of life, your longing will burn away the curtain of the ego separating you from the truth, and you will finally come to know who you are.

The Stepping-Stone

Do you hope to be worry-free? Don't worry that you have worries. Worry is a stepping-stone that allows us to grow. A life without worries and questions is a dead life.

We meditate to obtain peace of mind. Occasionally, people mistakenly believe peace of mind to be a state from which all worries have vanished.

Throughout our whole lives as humans, our worries won't cease. When one worry is resolved, a new one soon develops to take its place.

True peace of mind comes from an attitude of acceptance.

The living must worry, anyway. It's proof that we live. Worry about something for a while, and you'll come to a point where you make a choice. Try to put that choice into practice, and you'll find that greater worries and choices are waiting for you. That's life.

Once you reach some realization and conclusion through deep worry, your wandering ends and peace comes to you. At the same time, you realize the things you've been worried about were so trivial. And that's when greater worries begin.

Don't hope to be worry-free. Don't hope for an ocean without surging waves. Truly give your all to passionately walking the path of life your soul and conscience have chosen, and boldly embrace all worries coming to you on that path.

Encountering the One

On opening my whole body and mind and becoming one with true life, I encountered the One. The One is shining in my heart. The One is vibrating in my heart.

There was one who awakened, it is said, on hearing the sound of cattle calling in a silent field. The sound of a cow and her calf searching earnestly for each other, the sounds of their crying moo, echoing in the void, were like the earnest heart of this one searching for the truth.

When your search for the truth deepens and leads into prayer, you feel your earnest desire to find your lost divinity.

When your prayer grows deeper, you realize that divinity has also been earnestly seeking the humans that have grown distant from itself.

Then the prayer of the human becomes the prayer of the divine, and, when the two prayers meet as one, we feel deeply moved with our whole bodies.

Then we feel the divine nature dwelling in everything, and encounter the One in everything.

Live for Change

Though you live but a day, but an hour, you should live for the dreams, values, and spirit you have chosen. Don't live a habitual life, trained to the familiar and the comfortable. Through intense self-examination and ceaseless self-challenge, create change, and adjust your track toward growth and completion.

Am I now living the dreams and values I have chosen? Or am I living a formulaic, habitual life?

You should often take time to examine yourself and ask these questions. You should plan how you will create change for a better life, and you should put into practice and continue to live what you have planned.

If you live your life habitually, just letting day after day flow on by, then you cannot say that you have genuinely lived your life.

Will you live a productive, growth-oriented life, or a life maintaining the status quo? The answer is determined by your awareness, design, and practice.

Strictly speaking, there is no "status quo." For the status quo is a state of self-negation, a state from which your dreams and your genuine spirit have vanished.

If you look at this coolly, you'll see that it's more difficult to maintain the status quo. Try walking in place for a long time. It's harder and less interesting than walking normally.

Only if you go forward do your environment, your space, and the people you meet change; only then do you gain a new fascination for life, learning, and inspiration.

Only if you go forward can you move in a direction you desire. Don't complain, "Why doesn't my life change?" as you walk in place. If you live life habitually, without intense self-examination and reflection, you cannot make proper use of the time and space that have been given to you.

The Master of Your Brain

A purpose in life acts like a directional signal for the brain. The brain continues to process all information according to its light. Without that light, the brain cannot help but follow its survival instincts and habits. Those who have turned on their directional signal, their purpose in life, are the masters of their brains.

Noe: Brain

The body is an extension of the brain. The brain's neural network is spread throughout the body. The mind is also an action that takes place in the brain. There is no mind without the brain. In view of this, we can say that the brain is the self.

Yet there is something called "consciousness" that watches the state of the brain. Consciousness and the brain have a relationship like that of a driver and car. Just as we need a driver if we are to move a car, consciousness must be awake if it is to make good use of the brain.

If the consciousness observing our brain is awake, then we have a brain with a master; if that consciousness goes out, we have a brain without a master.

A masterless brain is easily ruled by emotion and led about passively by information. When I am conscious that I am the master of my brain, I can actively process emotion and information. I develop the insight to see my situation clearly, like when a light bulb is turned on in a dark room.

When the power of insight emerges, the master of the brain appears. The master intervenes in situations where the brain is about to process information according to primary survival instincts and habits, and enables it to make other choices.

Live as the master of your brain. Don't leave your brain to become a jumbled mess of countless emotions and bits of information.

Become the master of your brain. Watch the emotions and information arise, and intervene actively in its processing.

Move

Thoughts you feel as you act are living thoughts. Thoughts you think while you don't act are dead thoughts. Don't live within dead thoughts. Don't stop even for a moment while you live. Move.

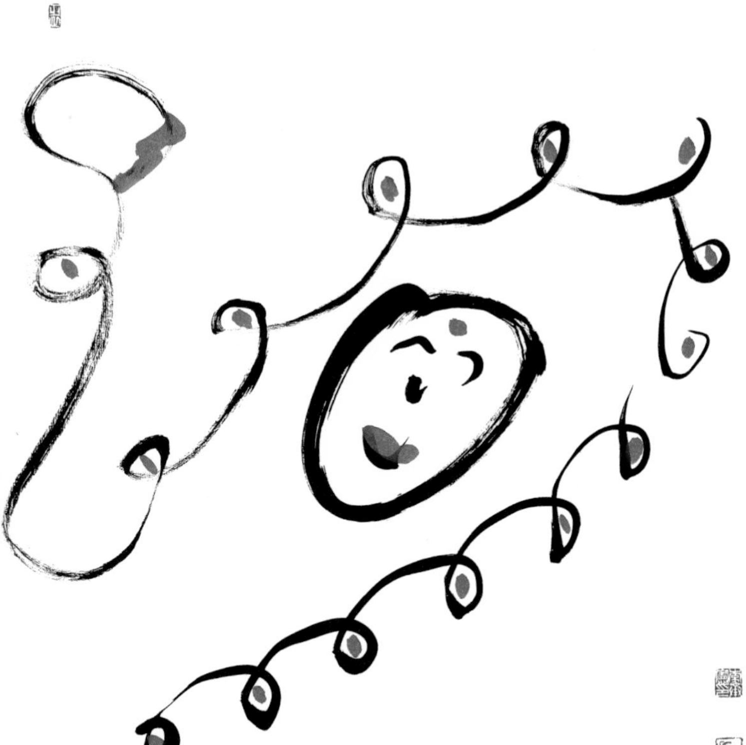

If you feel it's necessary, start—even if you aren't completely ready. Many people, when they start something, begin by debating whether they are ready. So they end up spending all their time only thinking.

When you feel the need, that is an opportunity. Then your timing is the best. If you have a need, move immediately.

Don't move after you're done thinking; think as you move.

If you dance, you'll feel more joyful. Just thinking isn't going to make you feel better. Think about how joyful you'll feel as you dance. Don't repeat the foolishness of putting off dancing as you debate whether dance will really bring you joy. We feel joy as soon as we dance. Everything is like that.

If you want to have fun, start doing something fun. If you want to be happy, start doing something that brings happiness. If you want to be healthy, start moving toward health.

Indra's Net

Nothing in this world exists in isolation. All life on the planet is connected through heaven, earth, and the empty space in between. From this knowledge emerges a heart of hongik, which seeks the good of all life.

Raise your right hand and look at your fingers. At first you'll see only your hand. Gradually move your eyes to your arm, shoulder, trunk, and entire body. Feel your body, which connects your limbs as one.

Now expand your field of vision to feel the empty space surrounding your body. Taking it further, try to feel the people, buildings, and nature around you in the same space.

The stars in the sky seem to be separated from each other, but they're connected as one through the void.

The maple and fig trees in my front yard are far enough from each other that the small leaves of one don't even brush against the big leaves of the other, but deep underground their roots are touching the same streams of water.

There is a very beautiful metaphor in the Hwaeom [Huayan] school of Buddhism. It is said that an endlessly wide, infinite, and transparent net, Indra's Net, is spread out in the palace of Jeseokchun, the land of the Buddha. Hanging from each knot of this net is a transparent jewel, and these jewels reflect clearly everything in the universe. Each jewel also reflects all the other jewels, so that a wave arising in any one spreads to all the others, and a sound coming from just one reverberates among all the jewels hanging from the net.

In a world of beings interconnected like Indra's Net, there is nothing unrelated to me. Each life is different from all others in all sorts of ways, but, in their essence, they are all interconnected.

In their source, all are one. People create differences from that one. And they end up confronting each other because of those differences. Since you and I are different, since you are not on my side, goes the insane logic they create, it's OK for me to harm you.

From knowing that all are one comes a heart of love for all.

The Seeker's Heart

Everyone has a desire to become one with the Tao; everyone has a seeker's heart. The Tao is the backdrop and driving force of everything existing in the world. We long for the Tao as a fish longs for the sea, for our lives are also a part of the Tao.

Do: Tao

You have probably had the experience of everything seemingly going well on the outside, until, one day, you suddenly felt as if your soul was empty. You will remember that feeling you had when you woke up in the middle of the night and stared off into space, unable to get much sleep.

Whether or not we're satisfied with our health, jobs, or personal relationships, right beneath the surface of our busy lives we always have the same questions.

What in the world does all this mean? Am I happy now? Does my life have some direction or goal?

You have no need to fear that moment. In moments when the roots of our lives are shaken, when we feel directionless, when feelings of emptiness rush over us, the desire to seek the Tao lifts its head within us. For the seeker's heart grows on the food of such feelings of emptiness and futility.

We all have a thirst to know something greater and more fundamental than our finite, temporary lives. We can't say exactly what it is, but we are always searching for something meaningful. That thing we cannot precisely identify is the Tao, and the desire to find it is the seeker's heart.

Consider precious the heart that asks fundamental questions of life. Love the mind that asks life, "Is this really all there is?" Keep digging into that mind.

Continue to develop a deep, pure thirst for the Tao, like a brooding hen. That thirst will grow and grow until it tears the veil of the concealing ego, and, like an arrow, pierces the heart of your soul. Then, as a chick breaks out of its shell, your eyes for seeing the truth will start to open.

LifeParticle Sun

Have you seen the light of the LifeParticle Sun?
Have you seen the light that shines even in the
blackest darkness? Have you seen the brilliant light
shining in its own radiance that no darkness can
harm?

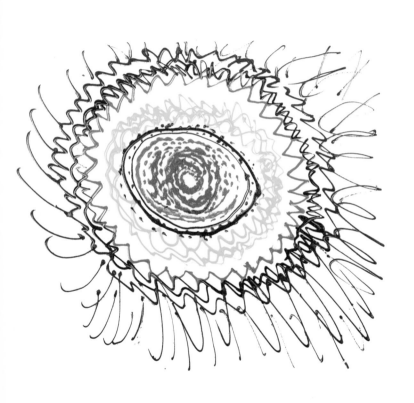

Light is who we really are.
Our substance is eternal life,
a complete, self-existent soul.

This is why our souls cannot be corrupted, cannot be hurt, and cannot be extinguished.

What appear to be depravity, injury, or extinction are merely traces of memory and experience obscuring the soul. These are merely shadows of the soul, never its substance. The soul itself is always pure and whole.

If we know a shadow is a shadow, we no longer fear it. However, if we think the shadow is real, it comes to dominate us and make us afraid.

Memories and wounds from the past aren't who we are. They are merely shadows. The substance of things long past has already disappeared. Are you, perhaps, controlled by those shadows?

As long as there is light, there is shadow. So don't hope for no shadows. You must see the shadows for what they are. And you must choose light.

The LifeParticle Sun is an expression of our essence, our light, and the root of our souls—great life and complete brightness.

Any memories or traces covering the soul disappear in the instant they meet the LifeParticle Sun, the root of the soul.

Encounter the LifeParticle Sun. Meet great life, the root of the soul. Encounter complete brightness, which cannot be harmed by anything.

Beating Heart

My heart is beating. Energy is flowing in my body.
I feel my life. It's beautiful and magical. What will I
do with this life?

Saeng: Life, being alive

I raise my right hand and place my left hand on my chest. Quietly controlling my breathing, I feel my heart.

This pulse, one of my body's most powerful vital phenomena, what makes this heart beat?

I sit alone, listening to the sound of my heart beating. The beating of my heart breaks through my body, spreading out into space.

If I were just alone, if there were nothing mysterious in the universe, would my heart beat on its own like this?

What is there that makes my heart beat so? What creates the beautiful colors of a newly bloomed flower? What makes the bird sitting on that spray of flowers sing?

Where did this life come from? Who am I, asking the meaning of life as I look at a beautiful flower?

I am just grateful as I listen to the sound of my beating heart. I pray for the happiness and well-being of everything with life as I listen to the sound of my beating heart.

May all that live be happy.

A Constant Mind

Everything in the world changes, but I believe there is something that doesn't change. I believe in the goodness and great love of the cosmos, which hopes for the growth and completion of life. Although I suffer from the many emotions I experience in life, I will never stop on my journey toward completion.

Hang Shim: Constant mind

Sadness, joy, loneliness, and other emotions are like movies projected on the screen of the mind. Just as the screen does not disappear when the movie is over, so, too, we have something unchanging amid the many emotions that come and go. We have something watching our anxiety, watching our sadness, watching our loneliness.

That something is our soul and true mind. Once we find that mind, we can develop the power to watch our emotions dispassionately instead of being led around by them.

What's important is realizing that we have the power to watch and control ourselves, and then working to develop that power.

If our minds are like a garden, then emotions are like the different flowers that bloom and wither in it all year round, according to the season. Emotions sometimes bring dynamism and significant change to our lives, but we must never be led around by them.

Don't be tossed about, floundering in waves of emotion. Learn how to surf emotions like waves.

Just as it is important to maintain good balance if you really want to surf well, so, too, only when we root ourselves solidly in our center, our soul, can we create our own lives with unshaken faith, even amid all life's changes, its ups and downs.

Pure Communication

I can feel your heart. I understand and love you. I
truly hope for your happiness and peace. Develop
this attitude toward everyone you meet, and you
will radiate loving energy.

Put your body in a peaceful state
so the energy of peace fills your mind.
Compassion develops from that peace,
and love wells up from within.

If you feel peace and love, you naturally
desire to share that peace and love with those
around you. If you develop that heart, then
accept and choose it.

Loving, peaceful energy goes out from
you in the moment you make up your
mind to share with those around you the
love and peace within.

If you meet people who have loneliness and
sadness, then share with them the energy
of love and peace within you. Give them
strength.

Energy is the most beautiful and purest form
of information. We cannot fully express in
words the beauty of a loving person's smile.
However, we can feel the energy of that love.

Loving people can feel the joy and sadness between them even without words. But when we are separated and do not love each other, we cannot feel another person's joy and sadness.

When we give and receive energy with open hearts, we communicate wordlessly. Then we cannot cause another person pain, because we feel it ourselves.

When the other person hurts, I hurt. For me to be at peace, I have to enable the other person to be at peace. For me to be happy, I have to make the other person happy.

When we recover a sensitivity for feeling our own energy, we can naturally feel the energy of others.

Through energy, we can experience communication with others, with nature, and with this whole universe on the purest, most fundamental level.

Ceaseless Growth

When we accept without resistance life's suffering and pain, we can experience life much more consciously. Experiencing life with an awakened consciousness is a shortcut to growth and the most wonderful spiritual teacher.

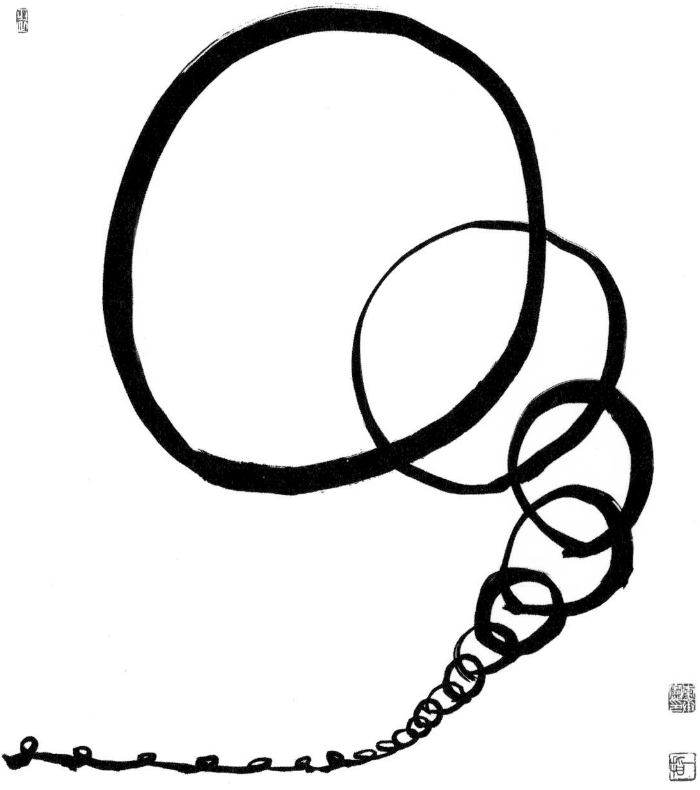

Our lives are ceaseless cyclical sequences of coming and going, rising and falling. If you want something newer and better, you must not resist this cycle of life.

Just as you can inhale again only if you exhale, you can accept the new only if you send away the old. Few who have soared to the heights they wanted in life have not spent time wandering in low places.

Learn to ceaselessly send away the old, lay down your attachments, and accept life rather than resist it.

Then you will see. Although today seems to pass exactly like yesterday, and you seem to always be living your life with the same worries and troubles, at some moment, you will discover that you have grown.

This is why, despite the sufferings and anguish that are an unavoidable part of life, we can ceaselessly go forward in our lives, waiting for tomorrow with faith and hope.

We can take one more step toward growth and completion as we experience life's coming and going, rising and falling, sometimes a fierce wind, sometimes a gentle breeze.

As you live with greatness in all the cycles of life, enter the deepest place of your being. Within, meet your noble self, beyond all the self-negation and desires.

Only when we accept completely the cyclical process of life can the pain and suffering we feel in life be reduced. And only then can we grow and develop ceaselessly, despite all those obstacles standing before us.

A Picture of the Soul

It is character that reveals the soul. Character is a picture of the soul seen through relationships. Although the soul is not visible to the eye, your character shows how much your soul has grown.

Hold precious everyone you meet. They are soul partners helping you on your journey to develop good character.

Just like you, other people are experiencing sadness, pain, and frustration in life, and they know that life isn't easy. They are working to discover the meaning of life, and they are learning and growing through experience, just like you.

Just like you, others have a thirst for the growth of their souls. When you understand the people who work and live with you to be partners in spiritual growth, you begin to have greater compassion and magnanimity, openness and gratitude.

Spiritual growth is a very social concept. Relationships and communities are the best schools for spiritual growth. The families, schools, and workplaces we each belong to are places of education through which we can grow. The people we meet there, and with whom we communicate, work, and live, are partners for spiritual growth.

Although we occasionally have conflicts, hurt others and are hurt, and experience pain in personal relationships, in each moment we work to be honest, sincere, and responsible. We examine ourselves and learn in those relationships. And by putting into practice what we've learned, we develop good habits.

Good character is developed by the coming together of good habits. Good character allows us to make good choices.

Through good choices, and the practice of those good choices, we become better people, and the world becomes a better place to live.

A Dream That Makes Your Heart Pound

A dream is your unique answer to how you should use your life. It is like a compass, giving direction to your ceaselessly moving life.

Shim: Mind

Life is a series of events. Between the two events of being born and dying, countless small events are interposed, creating the great event of life.

We are the planners and performers of this great event. Plans must be solid if this event is to be wonderful. The plans and scenario of the event called life are what we call dreams. Those who have dreams can stand boldly and confidently on the stage of their lives as the lead players in a drama they have written themselves. Then life becomes a wonderful event full of challenges and adventures.

Those who have no dreams stand awkward and unwilling onstage in a performance planned by someone else until the final curtain closes. Such lives, although they appear safe on the outside, are like some obligation that must be endured.

Have a dream. Life is not to be lived according to a set mold. Life is something you invent yourself, following an inner voice.

A dream is found within contemplation, worry, introspection. A dream doesn't just develop—it is created. What is it I truly want? What fills my heart with hope and joy? What do I want to live for, and how? Continue to question yourself seriously until you find your own answers.

The world is swamped by good words about happiness and success. However, these are merely other people's words. Don't live according to the thoughts and answers of others.

You should live as the master of your own life by questioning yourself, choosing for yourself, and doing your best to follow that choice.

Humans have the ability to choose the reason for their own existence and to create a life consistent with that choice. The joy of creation is known only to those who have a dream. Those with dreams can choose the lives they want to live. They learn how to be responsible for their choices, and they go on living, relishing the joy of true creation.

Your Luminous Soul

The sun shines when the clouds clear away.
The divine mind, luminous as the sun, seeks
 its own light.

Bohn Shim Bohn Tae Yang: The divine mind seeks its own light

We have within us a mind bright like the sun. It's hard to always maintain that mind, but it's very important to know that this mind is our true, eternally changeless form.

This is because, when you feel and know that this mind is there within you, you long for this mind, and are willing to search for it.

Our emotions and environment change constantly, like the seasons and the weather, but our souls are always there shining like the sun.

Knowing that you have a soul bright and clear like the sun, perceiving and feeling that soul, you will realize that it is very precious and beautiful. When you consider yourself important and precious, you will begin to feel the same way toward other forms of life and toward the world.

Our souls are truly beautiful. Each of us, having a beautiful soul, is truly precious. Open your eyes to yourself. Discover yourself and develop your value.

Even in the darkest despair and pain, be moved by and praise your noble soul, which recovers your mind, bright and shining like the sun.

Like the shining sun, let your bright soul illuminate the world.

The Source

That which feels everything happening within you,
that which judges all things—encounter that.

Han: The source

That consciousness has been watching you. That mind watches everything about you, although you don't know when it started watching. That mind is Han, the source.

Everything is clearly visible from the seat of han. You see all the emotions you feel, and even the roots of those emotions.

Your body and everything you have keep changing, but Han—your essence—does not change. The Changeless sees, hears, and feels everything.

It is important to know han because han is the source of creation. You can make good choices when you know han.

With nothing guaranteed, with everything uncertain, and with nothing working out as we intend, our very lives hold the seeds of tragedy and pain. Yet we can turn the tragedy of life into a blessing when we know han, when we see ourselves and make good choices from the center of han.

What's important is that we have the divinity and creativity that allow us to choose happiness and unhappiness.

Enlightenment is not some special state. It is a moment-by-moment choice, like light.

It is genuinely up to us whether we will be creators of life or bits of straw tossed about by waves on the ocean of life.

The roots of life are tragedy, but tragedy is changed into blessing by our choice when we encounter the Han within us and our divinity and creativity are expressed. Changing the tragedy of life into a blessing—that is the power and life of enlightenment.

Bird of the Soul

Your Bird of the Soul has built a nest in your heart.
Through good words, good thoughts, and good
deeds, give that bird greater wings. Turning your
Bird of the Soul into a Golden Phoenix, let it soar in
the vault of heaven.

Meetings are very important in life. Destinies, even, are sometimes determined through certain encounters. That's why, as we hope for good meetings for ourselves, we should always work to ensure that any meeting with us can be a good meeting for the other person, too.

But even more important than meeting with others is the meeting with ourselves: the encounter with our souls.

One good way to meet your soul is meditation. Another is keeping a journal.

Keep a journal for a while, and you'll find that you have honest talks with yourself. Then you genuinely encounter yourself by "crashing" against yourself.

Meetings that involve only brushing against each other do no good for either side. If you're going to meet another, do it with ferocity. This is even more important when your meeting is with yourself. See to it that sparks fly from your encounter with your soul; see to it that it produces a chemical reaction in your soul.

Those who keep a journal have many days on which they meet themselves. The more frequent those days, the less frequent are the days on which you have to worry about what others think of you. You will begin to develop a determination to live for your true self.

Keep a journal for a while, and you'll find yourself asking often: How did I spend my day today? How will I spend my day tomorrow? Those who keep journals never stop asking these questions until the day their lives are done. Again and again, they hone the basic skills of life: diligence, honesty, and integrity.

When I confess my heart to myself, and to heaven, once each day, when I write in my journal, it is a time of earnest prayer, no different from deep meditation.

True Life

True life surrounds our bodies, within and without, through the void. Money, knowledge, prestige, success, and the rest are merely the shadows of life. Take hold of the pulse of life; don't live clinging to life's shadows. Encounter true life.

Ki: Life energy

Compared to the infinite void, our bodies are small things, like dust. But our minds can feel the whole void and can easily embrace it.

Breathing correctly is the best way of feeling the void. Breathe each breath consciously for a while, and you'll come to understand that the source of your being is not your body, but the void itself.

Then you will perceive intuitively that your being is not restricted to the inside of your body or limited to the time you are alive.

When you breathe, don't try to put the void into your lungs; toss your entire body into it. The void is infinite. Don't try to use only that much of it that is the volume of your lungs. The void will comfortably surround and embrace your whole body once you toss your body into it.

Just as there is void outside our bodies, there is void inside, too. The two voids connect, which is why, if the great void outside the body is ailing, the small void inside also becomes sick.

The void enters and exits our bodies, helping us maintain life without discriminating between saints and sinners. Everything living is supplied with life from the void and depends on it.

The true God is not found in scriptures or churches or temples. He is found in the void. The void exists within all life, and the void is God, so every time a life disappears due to the carelessness of a human, it is like God losing a house in which to dwell.

The void is inside and outside our bodies; therefore, we are embracing God without and within. We can feel the mind of God, which fills heaven and earth, when we breathe correctly.

The void we feel through breathing will be a great freedom to the righteous and a prison to the unrighteous. God enters and exits our bodies whenever we breathe, so how can we breathe properly unless our attitudes are right?

The Greatness Within

When people have a great cause and dedicate themselves, giving everything they've got to achieving their purpose, heaven is moved and bestows upon them bright, numinous energy. Earth is moved, and builds for them connections that will bring happiness.

Dae Eui: Great cause

We all have a great mind. That mind wells up from self-existent, eternal life.

When that greatness awakens, we not only take care of our own personal interests but also develop a desire to be of infinite service toward great, important values.

When that mind awakens, we come to know a holy love that works for the good of all life. That mind lifts us up within trials and frustrations, giving us the gift of great ideals, passionate hearts, and indomitable will.

What did you do in the moment you realized the greatness within you? Did you acknowledge and choose it? Or did you deny it and go back to your old, comfortable ways?

When holy thoughts well up out of great life, we must have the eyes to see them, the courage to acknowledge and choose them, and the will to put them into practice. Considering those thoughts precious and devoting ourselves to developing them, we can create genuine change in our lives, in our neighbors' lives, and in the lives of humanity.

Recognize the greatness within you and use it to your heart's content. What's truly important is having profound respect for yourself.

When you respect and become immersed in yourself, the ideas and strength to realize inner greatness begin to emerge from that sense of oneness.

In the moment we sense our inner greatness and holiness, we feel heaven in our brains, and we hear the call of the Creator, who asks us to actualize our likeness with heaven. Boldly and proudly, answer the Creator's call.

The Law of Love

The human soul grows through love. It's important to realize that you can create love infinitely instead of wandering in search of someone to love you.

Love grows more greatly when you give it than when you receive it. This amazing fact is the Law of Love.

If you want to live a life full of love, first give it without striving to receive it. If you keep trying to get love, your love will constantly grow smaller.

Because you're trying to receive love, you will constantly feel sad and inadequate when the love you want doesn't come. You will become endlessly sadder and lonelier. And you will come to mistakenly believe that you don't have love yourself.

If you think about it quietly, you'll realize that you're happier when you give love than when you receive it. To use a knife as a metaphor, the one trying to get love holds a knife by the blade, while the one trying to give love holds the knife by the handle.

Those who keep trying to get love are anxious and worried. "What if my love leaves me?" they ask. "What if love never finds me?" On the other hand, people who give love to those around them have confidence.

Everyone has the power of love. If you want love, you must use love. If there is no one close you can give love to, then love yourself first. Once that love fills you, all you have to do is give it to others. That's how you begin.

There is love inside us. However, we can't experience that love unless we use it. We can't trust it unless we experience it.

Love is like a spring that never runs dry. The more we use it, the more new love arises.

One Mind

O greatness of mind. O mysteriousness of mind.
A person's pure, honest heart moves the hearts of
others, creating undreamed-of miracles.

Il Shim: One mind

"I still feel fear, even though I meditate enthusiastically. And my loneliness doesn't disappear, either. Why is that? Am I doing meditation incorrectly?" I sometimes get questions like these.

Whenever I get such questions, I say this: "It's extremely normal for you to be fearful, sad, and lonely."

As long as we live human lives in this world, such emotions will never disappear, no matter how much we meditate. What's important is that we have a mind capable of watching and controlling those emotions.

We can make new choices that bring more positive results in any situation because we have that mind.

Will you look at your sadness, loneliness, or fear and remain in that situation, saying, "That's just how I am"? Or, despite all that, will you choose a bright, clear mind and the power of the soul?

You cry because you're sad, then become sadder because you cry, and, because you cry more, become sadder still. Will you expand and reproduce that sadness? Or will you let go of that sadness and choose something else?

No matter how unfortunate your current situation, the true power of the mind can change that unhappiness into happiness. This is why we must always keep the fires of our minds burning.

If you turn on the light of your mind and concentrate, you'll develop courage in fear and discover the strength of brilliant solitude in loneliness.

We cannot surround ourselves only with the environments we want, but we can choose how we will react to our environments. Anyone can smile when things go well. Those who can smile when things don't go well know the true power of the mind. Seeing hope in despair, choosing the positive in a negative situation—this is the true power of the mind.

Heaven in the Brain

Your brain is the place heaven dwells. The infinite power of creation has descended into your brain. Choose that power and use it to your heart's content.

Chun: Heaven

We are connected with the divinity of the cosmos through our brains. That's why we use the expression, "God has descended into the brain." Here, God means the laws and infinite love of the universe, its infinite life force, not an object of faith.

We seek to become better beings and work to resemble heaven because heaven, the seed of divinity, has descended and dwells in our brains.

Our brains can become infinitely great because heaven is within them. Our brains, if we ask, can readily do things we have never done, even things we don't know about. Our brains have the great power to find a path where none is visible, and to make a path where none is to be found.

All the organs and cells in our bodies are connected with our brains. My brain is connected with other people, the earth, and the whole cosmos, as well as with my body.

That's why, when our spirits choose a vision, all our cells, the planet, and the cosmos learn of it through our brains. Then our brains become magic brains, pulling in all the information of the universe to achieve the vision we have chosen.

Don't be confined by the self you have experienced, the self you know. Going beyond what you know and what you have experienced, challenge your brain with new questions and give it new tasks—then it will begin to manifest infinite creativity.

You can invite anyone, anything, into your brain. You can encounter anyone, anything, in your brain. You can give your brain the gift of any vision at all.

And as long as you have a vision, you might as well invite into your brain the most beautiful, numinous thing in the world. Give your brain the gift of the greatest vision you can choose.

The Blessings of Life and Death

In the world of the finite body, death is the extinction of life and the end of everything. However, in the infinite world of energy, death is an illusion, and there is nothing but the cycle of life.

The waters of the river of life flow endlessly. No one knows when those waters began. And no one knows when they will end. The waters of that river flow endlessly, and our lives, too, flow on. But just as the waters of a river meet the sea, so, too, our lives, in the end, will meet an ocean.

People speak of it as the "Ocean of Death." For those who know energy, though, it is the "Ocean of Life." It is a beautiful sea filled with infinite life energy. Life is not a voyage to the Ocean of Death, but a journey to encounter the Ocean of Life.

When you awaken to the world of energy, you realize that even the death that comes after life is another extension of life. Death is not the end, but a new beginning and birth.

The human body and soul, with death, welcome another birth. The body is reborn as countless other lives in the great cycle of nature, and the soul returns to the source whence it came. Energy, the source of life, is not extinguished with death; it simply moves.

The moon waxes and wanes with the size of earth's shadow, but the moon itself remains a sphere, unchanged. When the darkness of night comes after the setting sun, which has shone its bright light on all things during the day, the sun itself is still shining on the other side of the globe. In the same way, human life is merely marked by the phenomena of life and death.

Just as with life, death is a beautiful gift. Since we know that our physical life is finite, we struggle to overcome the transience of existence brought by death. We have developed a thirst for eternal truth because death exists, and we have come to know the world of energy and the soul linking life and death. So death is a mechanism for enlightenment and a blessing for the completion of the soul.

We have been given the blessing of life and the blessing of death. We have no reason to worry or be anxious, for we have the void, the eternal world of energy to which we will one day return.

Rooted in the void, a brilliant vision in our hearts, we live resolutely in the eternal now.

For the Good of All

The heart that seeks to go beyond its own narrow interests to work for the greater good of other people and life—this is the most precious value of humanity, and the greatest function of the human brain.

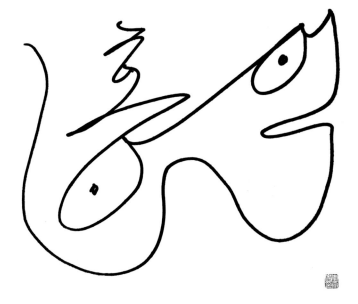

Hongik: Benefit all

Regardless of what sorts of lives we have lived so far, or what kind of people we believe ourselves to be, we all want to be remembered as people who contributed something to the world.

Somewhere deeper than our victim consciousness, selfishness, and arrogance, somewhere deeper than our instinct to find sensory pleasure, all human beings have a Hongik instinct: we want to do something good for the world.

The Hongik instinct is the fundamental power that caused us to enter the world and the driving force that enables us to keep going, even when weary and troubled. When this Hongik instinct is not fulfilled, we feel somehow empty even after we've finished a busy day's work, and we have regrets about our lives when we end our time in the world.

Somewhere deep in our hearts lives a noble desire to do good for the world. This is the seed of divinity planted deep within us.

Each of us has a dream. And we hope that dream will not stop at the pursuit of our personal profit, but will contribute to our families and neighbors, and, furthermore, to all of society and the human race.

No matter where we work or what kind of jobs we have, no matter whom we work with as we live our lives, deep in our hearts we want to be people who strive to do good for the world. We are originally Hongik humans.

Our Bright Conscience

Within us is a bright mind and conscience. Despite all the weak points people have, and all the evil they do, people are our hope because all of them have consciences.

Yang Shim: Conscience

The conscience is our bright inner light that cannot be hidden and cannot be ignored—our complete knowing.

Because we have a conscience, we know that we have done wrong when we have done wrong, we know that we have lost balance when we have lost balance, and we can recover uprightness.

A wise person does not believe in and rely on anyone else, but illuminates her own conscience and judges, chooses, and acts according to it.

When we rely on our bright conscience, we, alone, are clean and bright. We don't need to rely on anything else.

When we are ignorant of the strength of the conscience within us, we long for the light of the sun even while standing in its rays, and we foolishly wander in search of the light of fireflies.

The conscience is the brightest even of bright things, which reveals the truth by shining on everything in the world.

When we listen to our conscience, and when we have the faith that others will follow their consciences as we follow ours, we can realize true human value and dignity.

A Dance of Life

Countless people do a dance of life on this beautiful earth. Their hearts overflow with excitement, and the energy of Hongik, love for the good of all, surrounds the globe. The LifeParticle Sun shines in the sky.

Imagine that you received this question at the last bend in the road of your life: "Did you live a good life?" What would you base your answer on? Answering would be difficult without a standard to judge by.

The ultimate purpose in life for all human beings is the growth of their consciousness and the completion of their souls.

And each, in her own way, continues to realize this goal through the work she has chosen, her personal relationships, and her diverse life experiences.

In the end, there is one ultimate answer concerning the purpose of life, but it is up to each of us to realize and experience it.

Therefore, the goal of life is the same and yet different for each of us.

Who am I? What is the purpose of my life? What is your answer to these questions? If growth of your consciousness and completion of your soul comes to mind without any hesitation, then you're definitely ready now to lead an authentic life. All that remains is for you to live the answer you have found.

Divinity

When your love with yourself deepens, your love
with divinity begins. Love for the world springs up
from love with divinity. Since heaven is me, earth is
me, and since you and I are all one, the objects of
love stretch out to infinity, and there ends up being
nothing I do not love.

The greatest treasure in life is awakening to the truth that our true self is one with the great life force of the cosmos, and then opening ourselves wide to that stream of divinity.

That divinity, although exactly the same in everyone, is felt or not felt depending on whether we have open hearts that earnestly desire it.

To obtain deep wisdom and insight in life, more than anything else, we must have absolute certainty that we are guided by the divinity within us.

Many people live dark, powerless lives without hope because they do not know that they have divinity within them. Those who feel and know that they have a divine nature inside them discover a power of love and peace that can overcome all the darkness of life.

When we realize deeply that we are one with this power of infinite peace, our minds are not shaken and we remain aloof from the trivial things that once made us anxious and angry.

When we are one with the divinity within us, we can see the same divinity in others.

Then we are granted the beautiful attitude of ceaselessly devoting ourselves to make the lives of others, and our own, happier.

Even with Sunspots, the Sun Shines

Although we all have dark spots, we are all, at the
same time, the sun. Though it has sunspots, the
sun shines its light on the universe. We have many
human weaknesses, but our divine nature shines
like the sun despite all those things. We can love
and practice Hongik through the power of that
divinity.

Once you start watching your unfiltered self, it can occasionally be very painful. To grow, however, you need the courage to look unflinchingly at who you really are.

We first must learn how to be pure and true like young children. The truth has power because it is truth, no matter how small or insignificant.

Once you face the truth, you needn't be troubled, even if it's not what you wanted to see. Cheerfulness and strength are not the only things we have inside us.

Much that is dark and many weaknesses are in there, too. It's courageous to look at that darkness and those weaknesses without adding or subtracting anything.

We grow humbler when we can look at our inadequacies. We must first become true if we would truly grow. All we have to do is begin with those truths, no matter how small they may be.

Don't be a fake, trying to look bigger and better to others. Instead, strive to be genuine, even if in small ways. All you have to do is become a little genuine, and then gradually develop that truth.

Our innocence is pure gold, requiring no plating. Don't waste your precious time and life gilding yourself; such a coating is bound to fade sooner or later, no matter how solid and magnificent it may appear.

True Blessings

Let your smile, each word you speak, each motion
of your body be a blessing for yourself and the
world. Let the world be a more beautiful place
because you exist.

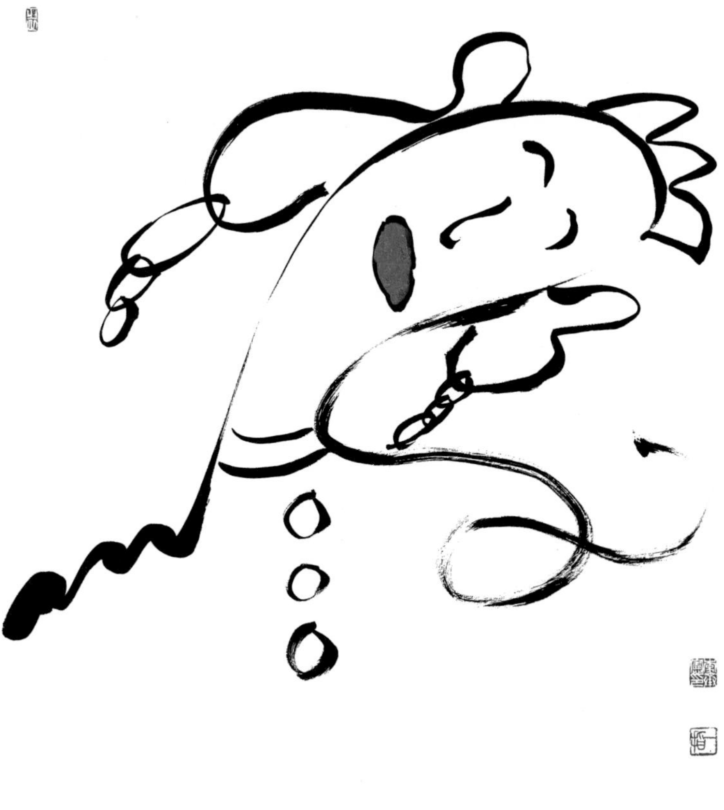

If you mention "enlightenment," many people will bring to mind a state of extreme peace and happiness, free of any pain, and mysterious spiritual abilities.

Enlightenment, however, means loving and accepting unconditionally even pain, which is one of the phenomena of life, as well as peace and happiness.

That's why enlightenment brings us great worries in place of life's little worries, which it takes away.

The enlightened worry more about the problems of the world than about their own problems, and their longing for the well-being of all life grows deeper, making the suffering of all people, all creatures, and all things their own. This is a gift brought by enlightenment, which, at the same time, brings deep anguish.

Though you awaken, you are troubled by life's many emotions. If there's a difference, it's that although you experience all those things, you're not swept away by them.

You feel that there is something inside you that keeps you from being shaken or swept away by the phenomena you experience, as if you are sitting quietly deep in the ocean, watching waves overhead that sometimes rage fiercely and sometimes roll gently.

Nowhere in the world is there an enlightenment that takes away all pain.

There is only an enlightenment that keeps you from being swept away by suffering, an enlightenment that enables you to discover blessings even in pain, an enlightenment through which your passion for sharing with the world the blessings you've discovered melts away the anguish of life.

Change Your Destiny

If you would change your destiny, first you must truly want to. What you do not want does not happen. Earnestly wanting something becomes intention. A solid intention leads to passion. Action follows passion, and ceaseless action changes destiny.

Gae Woon: Changing destiny

To change your destiny, first you must understand that yours is an existence you can choose. You must have the realization:
I choose my own value.

We all have absolute value that cannot be damaged by anything. We must feel our own innate, absolute value.

Some special inspiration or miracle is unnecessary for changing your destiny. What's important is determining your own path, choosing it, and then resolving to follow it, with a healthy intelligence and conscience. It's about putting into practice your choice and resolution honestly, sincerely, and responsibly.

If you want to change your destiny, never blame others. Those who take responsibility create changes that overcome problems. Change is already beyond you once you start blaming others. If you've dreamed of blaming others, then you should guard against it to such an extent that you shiver at just the thought of such a bad dream.

You must show the maturity to take responsibility for your choices and decisions. Most pitiable are those who put off on others the choices they should make themselves, and who seek in others the causes for their own failures. There can be no change or growth for such people.

Whatever you do, it's vital that you've chosen and decided on it for yourself. If, on my way up a mountain, a single, common pebble catches my attention, and I assign special meaning to it, then it becomes precious. That stone could be more precious to me than gold, even though it's nothing to other people.

Today is a very good day. Why is that? It's a good day because I decided it was a good day. By choosing it to be so, I've turned today into a good day.

Changing your destiny is like this.

World of Oneness

From the realization that all are one, a desire to heal the world develops, love for all life arises, and a means to create that love is achieved.

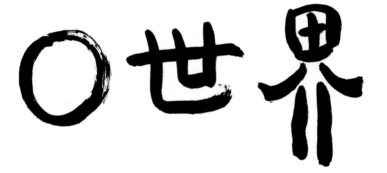

Han Se Gye: One world

There is a flame burning deep in our hearts. Although we don't know when or where it began, there is a flame blazing brightly.

That flame cannot be put out no matter how hard we try, and it cannot be damaged by anything. The flame is our divine nature; it is the "One."

The One is eternal, self-existent life without beginning and without end. It points to the source of existence from which all things arise and to which all things return. The history of the self that we believe is extinguished with our bodies also, with the One, has no beginning and no end.

Those who awaken to the meaning of the One know that, just as their lives are rooted in the One that is the source of being, so, too, are the lives of others. They come to realize that we are all one life in one community within one spirit.

When we awaken to the meaning of the One, we can see that the image of ourselves as separate individuals is an illusion, and we can see ourselves, all life-forms, and everything else that exists as flowers blooming on the one tree of Life.

We are able to see a world in which, although all are one, they are also different from each other, and in which, despite that, their source is also one.

Those who have awakened to the fact that nothing in the universe exists in isolation will choose lives lived for the benefit of all life.

People of Light

The seven jewels of light in your body, your chakras, come alive. Delight arises from deep within your mind. Its energy spreads to your whole face, making it bright and cheerful. Your hands float, moving on their own as they do a dance of the soul. O people of light, you are beautiful!

There is no reason to have a cheerful expression on your face. You're not wearing a cheerful expression because you feel good. You just do it unconditionally.

Let the light in your eyes be bright, peaceful, and overflowing with love and confidence. Let it be the greatest light you can create. Control the light of your eyes with the power of your brain.

You can create peace and love in your brain. Emit that peace and love with your whole face. Let your eyes shine with positive energy. Create a light in your eyes and an expression on your face so cheerful that it makes those around you wonder, Why is that person so happy?

Straighten your lower back and open your chest. Let all seven chakras open up and gush the energy of infinite life. Make your posture confident, bold, and proud.

Plant a beautiful dream in your brain. Create for yourself positive energy, making the light of your eyes gentle and peaceful.

Create good news each and every day. Good news makes good brains. Live always in positive thinking. Positive thoughts create miracles.

There is no hope in despair. There is no hope in conflict. Don't choose despair or conflict; choose hope in every situation. Hope is a choice.

Those who have hope and those who give hope are beautiful. Life is accompanied by much pain, but it shines in the moment you have hope.

Hope does not make the suffering of life itself disappear, but suffering has meaning when we have hope. Great hope makes even suffering beautiful.

Becoming Heaven

By knowing that there is a pure, precious soul within me, and by living a life encouraging that soul to grow, I finally become one with the heaven, the divinity, within me. The soul within a person growing to become one with the divine—this beautiful transformation we call Chunhwa.

Chunhwa: Becoming heaven

Human beings have a physical life, a social life, and a spiritual life. These are intimately interconnected, and we enjoy true health when all three kinds of life force are flourishing.

To develop the physical life force, suitable exercise, nutrition, rest, and play are needed. More important than anything else, though, is the understanding that my body is not me, but mine. When we have such an understanding, we can use our bodies' functions and energy as we desire rather than being led about by our bodies.

Social life force is obtained by realizing our own existential value in our relationships. When we fulfill our roles and responsibilities with honesty and integrity and contribute to our neighbors and society, we obtain the trust of those around us, which invigorates our social life force.

Spiritual life force develops when we comprehend that our bodies and personalities are not all there is to us, that we are spiritual beings.

When, based on this realization, we practice peace, harmony, love, and the original character of the soul, our spiritual life force grows.

No matter how healthy or socially successful we may be, unless we are filled with spiritual life force, our lives lose meaning and passion. This is because we are essentially spiritual beings and have a thirst and will for the completion of our souls.

The soul is a wholeness existing inside us. We have such a wholeness, and we have a will to reach out and touch that wholeness. That's why we can finally become one with divine nature.

Like caterpillars transforming into butterflies, all people can discover the great, holy souls inside them and lead lives for their souls' completion.

However, this only happens with conscious realization. To live a life of Chunhwa, you must know that you have a soul within you, and you must choose to embody the values of that soul every single moment.

Because...

Everyone has a natural yearning for completion,
we are able to change and recreate ourselves
endlessly. Due to that beautiful yearning,
we can become greater at any time.

About the Author

 Ilchi Lee is the author of the *New York Times* bestseller *The Call of Sedona: Journey of the Heart*, as well as *Change: Realizing Your Greatest Potential* and thirty-five other books.

A visionary and educator, he has dedicated himself to teaching energy principles and developing innovative methods to nurture the full potential of the human brain.

A nature lover, he lives in Sedona, Arizona's beloved red rock country and travels around the world to share his dreams and ideas. He invites readers to visit his website at www.ilchi.com and his digital learning platform at www.ChangeYourEnergy.com.